Introduction

Hello, My name is Briana Battle
I created this Journal to encourage, uplift, and inspire women to love themselves and learn about self-love. Nowadays, women tear each other down and disparage each other, rather than uplifting each other. It is also rare that you hear Women speak on self-love. I am a WOMAN with a VISION to EMPOWER WOMEN to DO MORE, SEE MORE, & BE MORE. I strongly believe that WOMEN should EMPOWER each other instead of being HATEFUL & ENVIOUS of one another. Other WOMEN are not my competition; I STAND with them NOT against them.

Ms. Briana

Self Love is the Best Love

Copyright ©2020 by Briana Battle
All rights reserved. This book or any portion thereof may not be reproduced or used in any manner whatsoever without the express written permission of the author except for the use of brief quotations in a book review.

Printed in the United States of America Book.
First Printing 2020
Second Printing 2024
ISBN - 978-1-943284-89-4
A2Z Books Publishing Lithonia, GA 30058
www.A2ZBooksPublishing.net
Manufactured in the United States of America
A2Z Books Publishing has allowed this work to remain exactly as the Publisher & Author Intended.

Happiness

N	F	L	A	U	G	H	L	E	E	L	J	E	O
N	E	I	T	M	E	R	R	Y	R	Y	J	O	Y
E	N	L	N	B	G	O	F	N	T	A	Y	R	R
O	E	N	E	E	L	C	H	E	E	R	G	H	I
D	V	P	T	P	A	E	S	M	I	L	E	E	I
E	I	L	N	Y	D	O	R	C	F	U	N	A	S
L	T	E	O	R	T	O	D	L	P	G	E	V	S
I	I	A	C	L	A	I	E	E	P	P	S	E	E
G	S	S	H	E	L	P	C	G	R	L	E	N	N
H	O	U	T	A	S	U	T	I	L	E	A	D	D
T	P	R	I	A	E	R	E	U	L	E	Y	Y	O
O	C	E	I	L	L	T	O	I	R	E	E	L	O
R	P	A	R	A	D	I	S	E	S	E	F	L	G
N	U	A	E	S	D	S	S	I	L	B	R	D	E

SMILE   RAPTURE   CONTENT   GOODNESS
DELIGHT   GLEE   JOY   CHEER
GLAD   LAUGH   PLAY   PLEASURE
PARADISE   FELICITY   POSITIVE   HEAVEN
FUN   BLISS   MERRY

"

Self-love

is extremely important in everyone's life.
So many times we forget how important
self-love is,
so don't ever forget this.

Ms. Briana

Self-love Questionnaire:

1. **What are your self-love goals?**

_____

_____

_____

2. **How do you plan to dedicate time to self-care?**

_____

_____

_____

3. **What are your boundaries and limitations?**

_____

_____

_____

Self-love Questionnaire:

4. What do you like to do?

_____
_____
_____
_____

5. What do you not like to do?

_____
_____
_____
_____

6. What are your life expectations for yourself?

_____
_____
_____
_____

Self-love Questionnaire:

7. What is your daily motivation?

8. Do you plan to put yourself first? How?

> *Self-love* needs to be a daily practice and put into your regular routine.

Ms. Briana

Self-Love Notes

(Write yourself a Love Note)

_____

_____

_____

_____

_____

_____

_____

_____

_____

_____

_____

"*Self-love* is about Loving Yourself.

Ms. Briana

 Notes

(Write yourself a Love Note)

_____

_____

_____

_____

_____

_____

_____

_____

_____

_____

_____

> **Self-love** is about putting yourself first and knowing your worth.
>
> **Ms. Briana**

Self-Love Notes

(Write yourself a Love Note)

_____

_____

_____

_____

_____

_____

_____

_____

_____

_____

_____

_____

> *Self-love* is Catering to Your Needs, Wants & Desires.

Ms. Briana

 Notes

(Write yourself a Love Note)

> ## *Self-love*
> is loving yourself
> in spite of your flaws.
>
> **Ms. Briana**

Self-Love Notes

(Write yourself a Love Note)

> *Self-love* is discovering your true self.
> **Ms. Briana**

 # Notes

(Write yourself a Love Note)

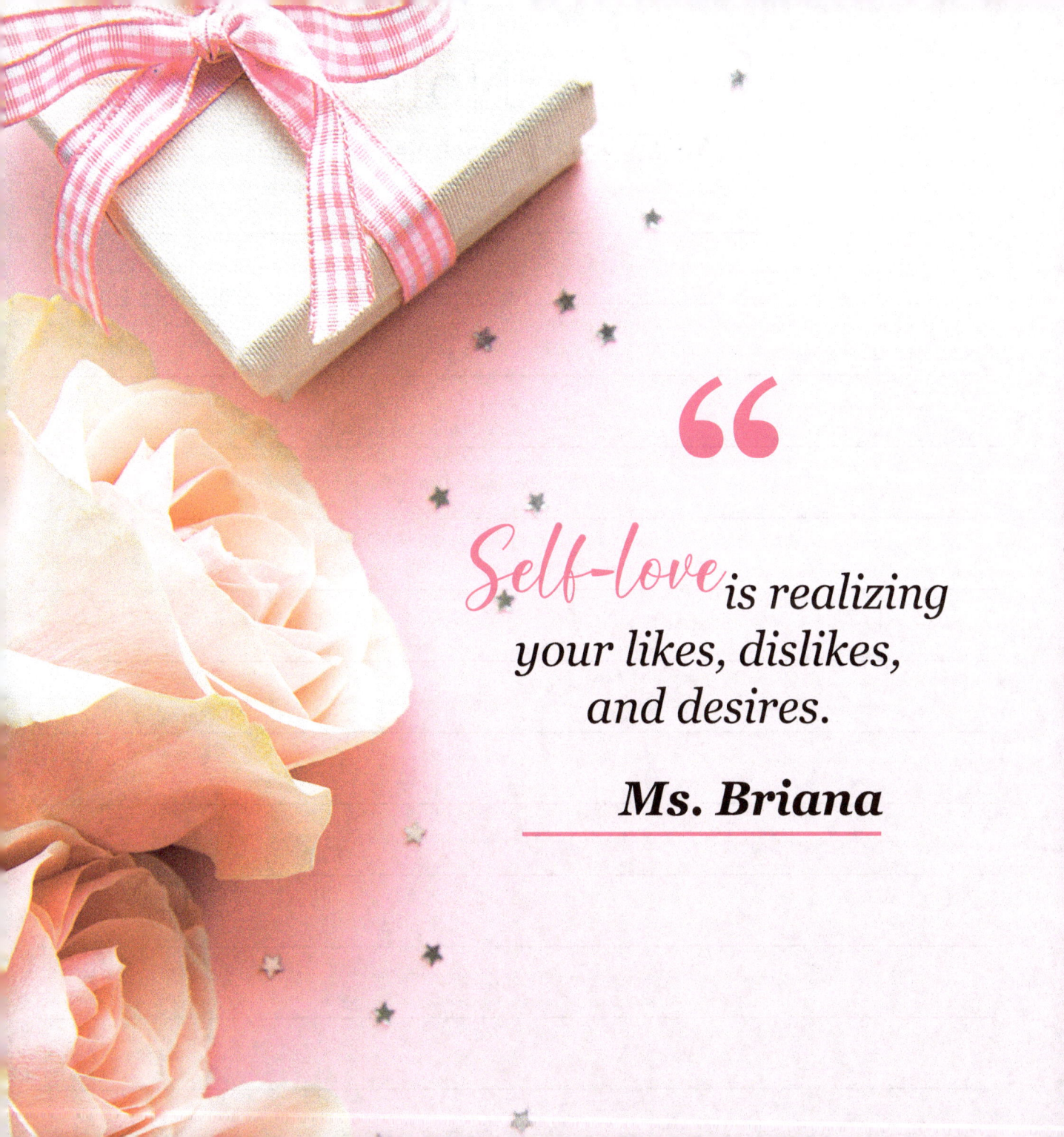

Self-Love Notes

(Write yourself a Love Note)

> ## *Self-love*
>
> is owning your past mistakes and forgiving yourself and never punishing your future for the past. Forgive yourself, grow from it and let it go. Your relationship with yourself sets the tone for every other relationship you have. Falling in love with yourself first doesn't make you vain or selfish. It makes you indestructible.
>
> **Ms. Briana**

 Notes

(Write yourself a Love Note)

_____

_____

_____

_____

_____

_____

_____

_____

_____

_____

Write 5 Ways You Can Show Yourself Self-Love

1.

2.

3.

4.

5.

Am I Showing Myself Self-Love?

☐ YES   ☐ NO

If I answered yes, how do I show myself self-love?

If I answered no, what changes do I need to make to ensure I am showing myself self-love.

Self-Love Calendar

(Use this Calendar to Track your Self Love Journey). You can add spa treatments, hanging out with friends, and even grabbing a cup of coffee and taking a walk at the park.

MONTH:

SUN	MON	TUE	WED	THU	FRI	SAT

> *Self-love*
>
> is knowing your limits and putting yourself first instead of settling for less or staying in your comfort zone.

Ms. Briana

Self-Love Notes
(Write yourself a Love Note)

> *Self-love* is building yourself up every morning and every night before bed. You shouldn't wait for someone to build you up just to turn around and tear you back down. You should build yourself up and celebrate you even when others don't celebrate you.

Ms. Briana

Self-Love Notes

(Write yourself a Love Note)

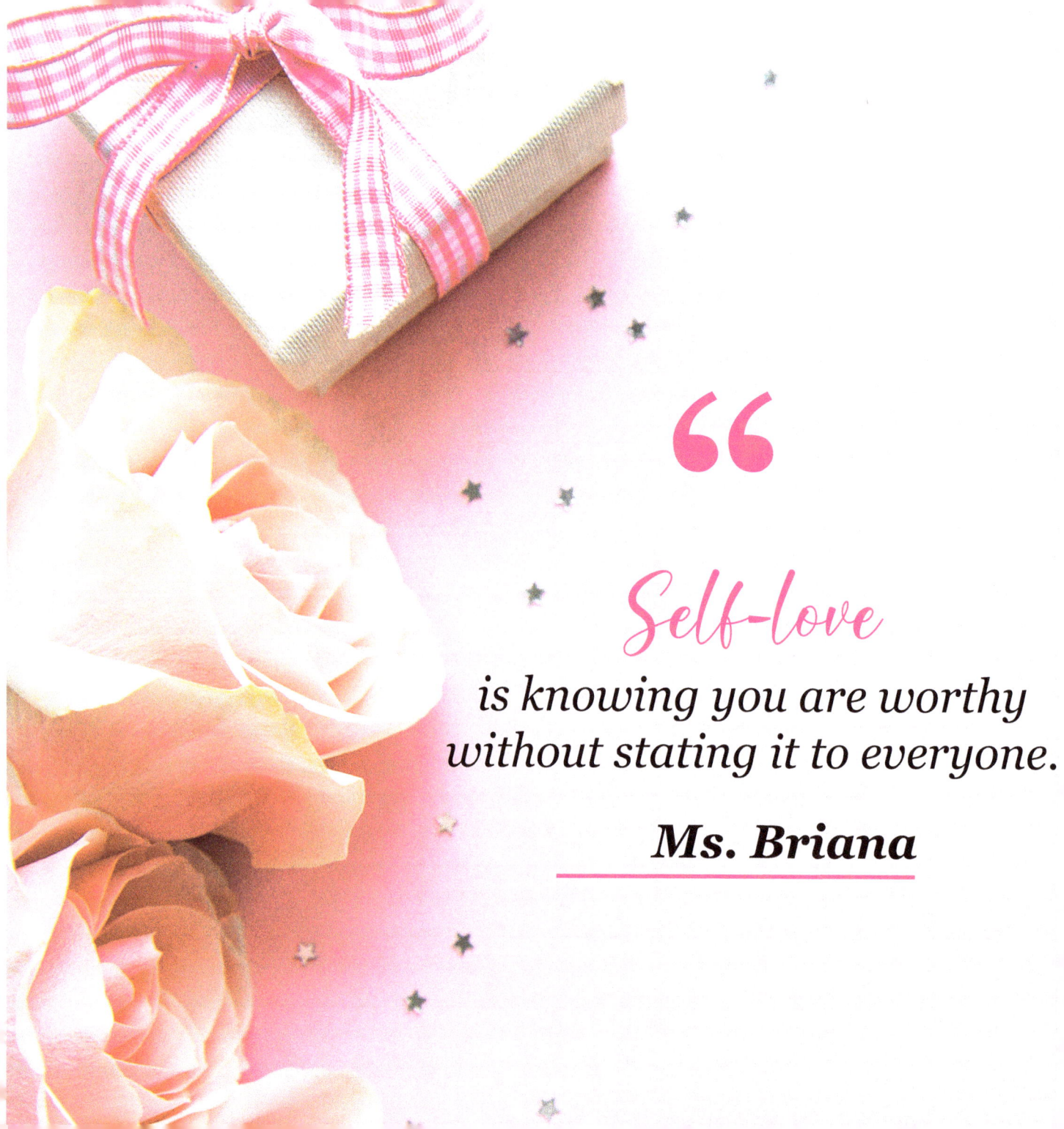

> **Self-love** is knowing you are worthy without stating it to everyone.
>
> **Ms. Briana**

Self-Love Notes

(Write yourself a Love Note)

_____

_____

_____

_____

_____

_____

_____

_____

_____

_____

_____

Self-love is accepting yourself.

Ms. Briana

 Notes

(Write yourself a Love Note)

_____

_____

_____

_____

_____

_____

_____

_____

_____

_____

_____

> *Self-love* is being yourself instead of trying to please others so you can fit in.

Ms. Briana

 Notes

(Write yourself a Love Note)

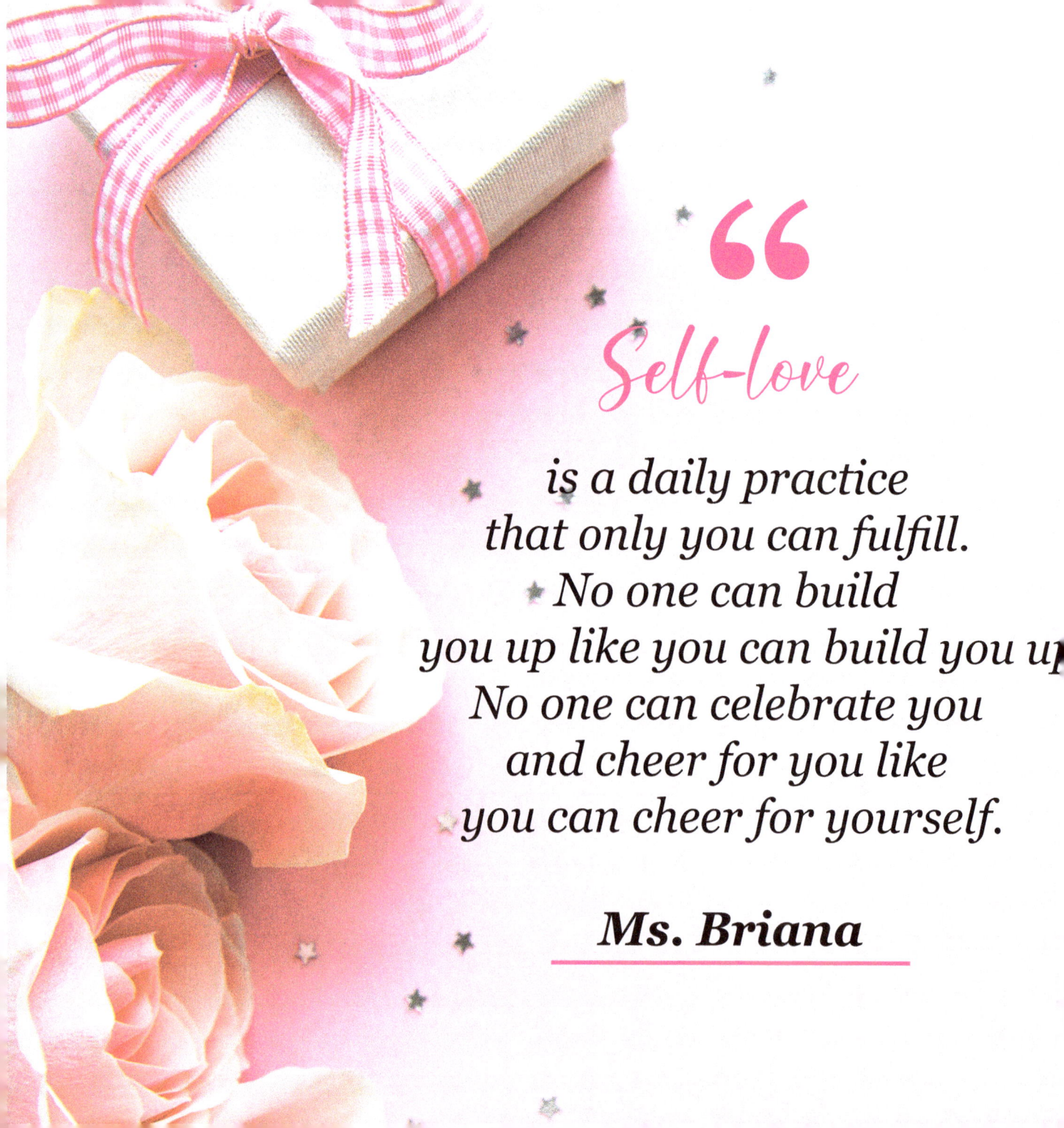

 Notes

(Write yourself a Love Note)

_____

_____

_____

_____

_____

_____

_____

_____

_____

_____

"

Self-love

is knowing that you're ENOUGH!

Ms. Briana

Self-Love Notes

(Write yourself a Love Note)

> ## *Self-love*
>
> is embracing your value, talents, and strengths. Don't rely on someone else for your happiness and self-worth. You are the only one responsible for that. If you can't love and respect yourself how can you possibly expect someone else to do that.
>
> **— Ms. Briana**

Self-Love Notes

(Write yourself a Love Note)

Write 5 Ways You Can Show Yourself Self-Love

1.

2.

3.

4.

5.

Am I Showing Myself

☐ **YES**   ☐ **NO**

If I answered yes, how do I show myself self-love?

If I answered no, what changes do I need to make to ensure I am showing myself self-love.

Self-Love Calendar

(Use this Calendar to Track your Self Love Journey). You can add spa treatments, hanging out with friends, and even grabbing a cup of coffee and taking a walk at the park.

MONTH:

SUN	MON	TUE	WED	THU	FRI	SAT

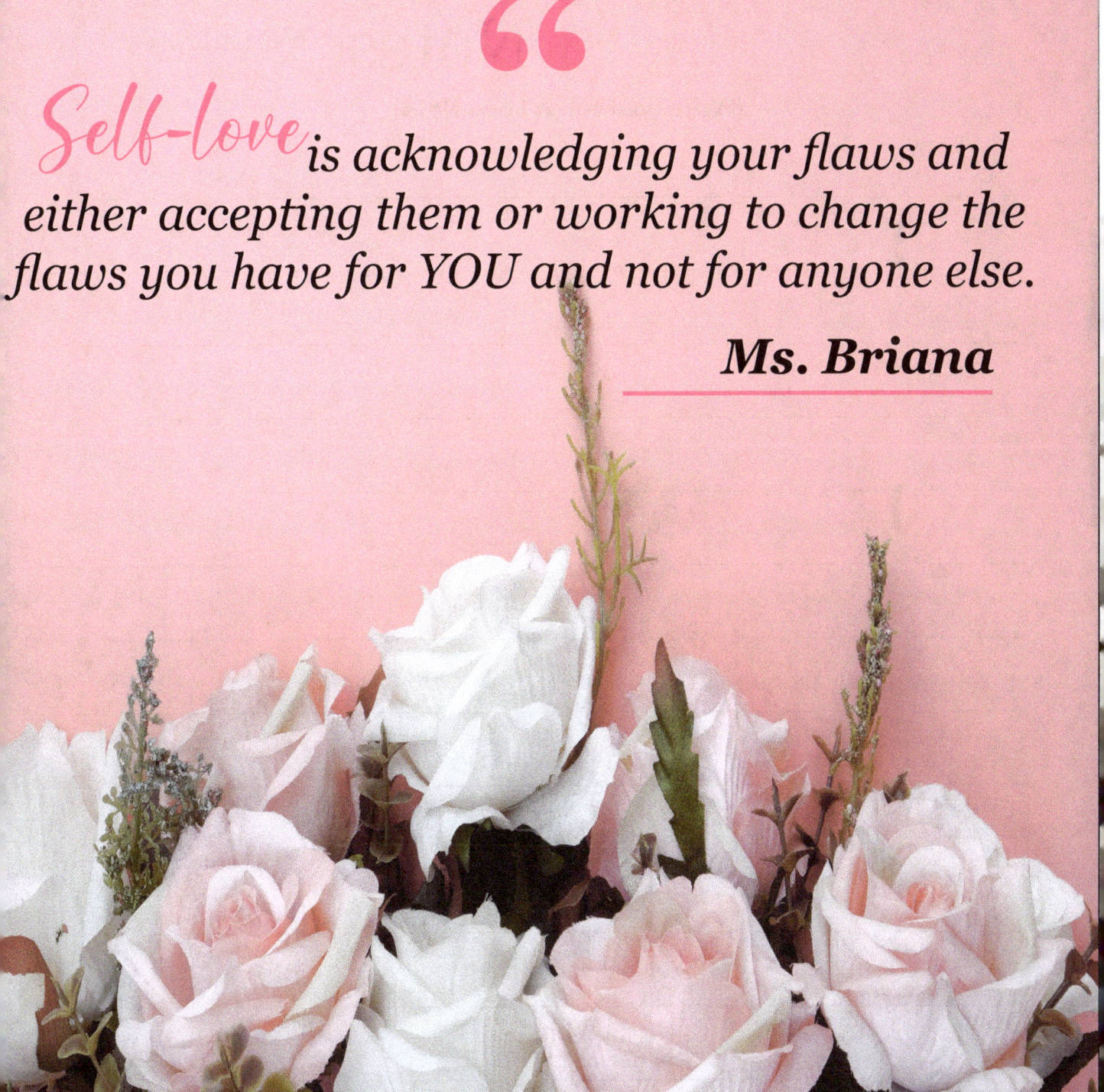

> *Self-love* is acknowledging your flaws and either accepting them or working to change the flaws you have for YOU and not for anyone else.
>
> — Ms. Briana

Self-Love Notes

(Write yourself a Love Note)

> ## *Self-love*

is acknowledging that you are perfect in spite of your imperfections. Every morning you should manifest into yourself " I am enough, I am beautiful, I am unique, I am different, I am awesome, I am amazing, I am proud of who I am and I love myself.

Ms. Briana

Self-Love Notes

(Write yourself a Love Note)

> ## *Self-love*
> is putting yourself first and never settling for less than you deserve.
>
> **Ms. Briana**

Notes

(Write yourself a Love Note)

> *Self-love*
> is not allowing people
> to run over you like a doormat.

Ms. Briana

 Notes

(Write yourself a Love Note)

_____

_____

_____

_____

_____

_____

_____

_____

_____

_____

_____

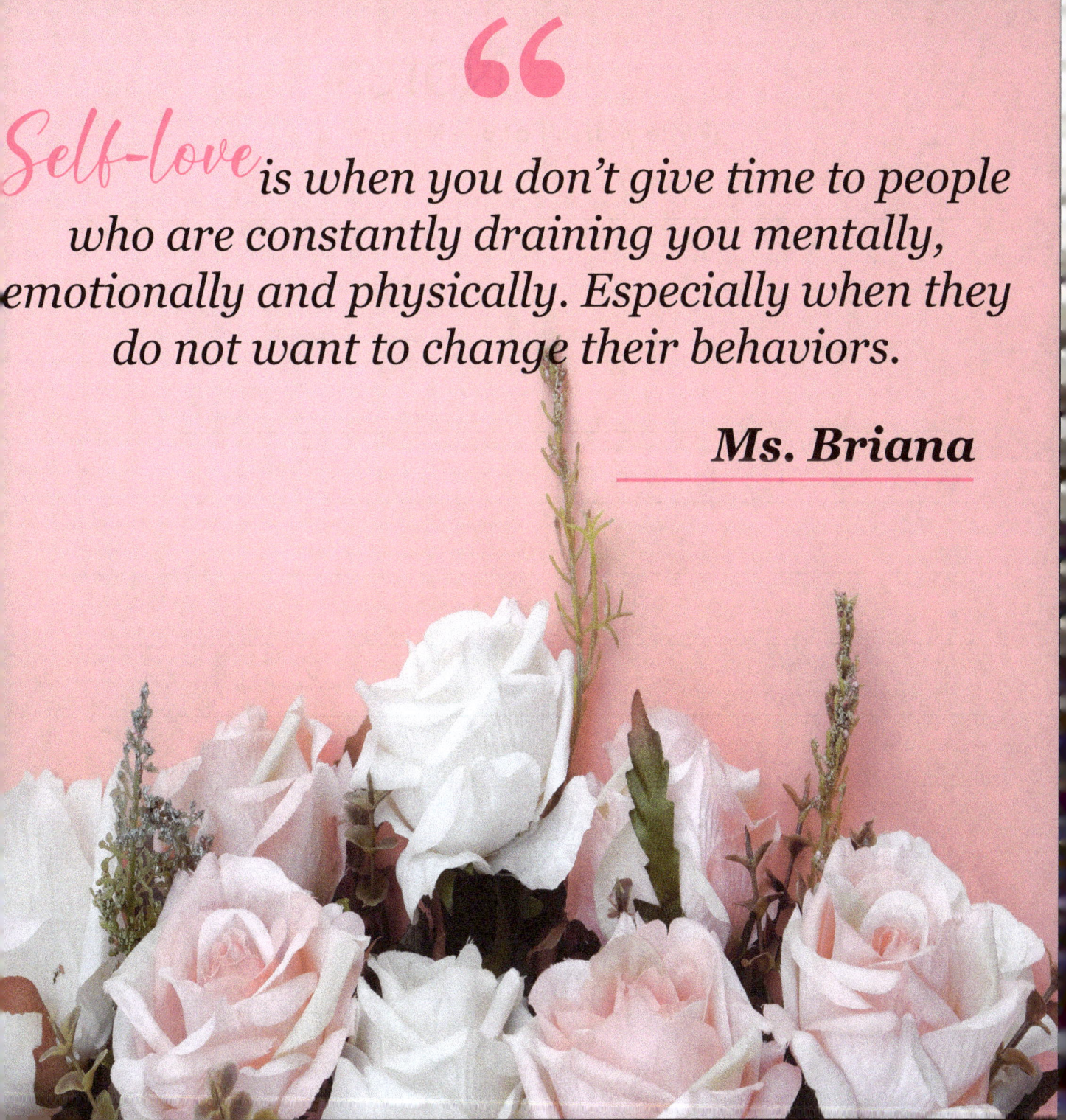

 # *Self-Love* Notes

(Write yourself a Love Note)

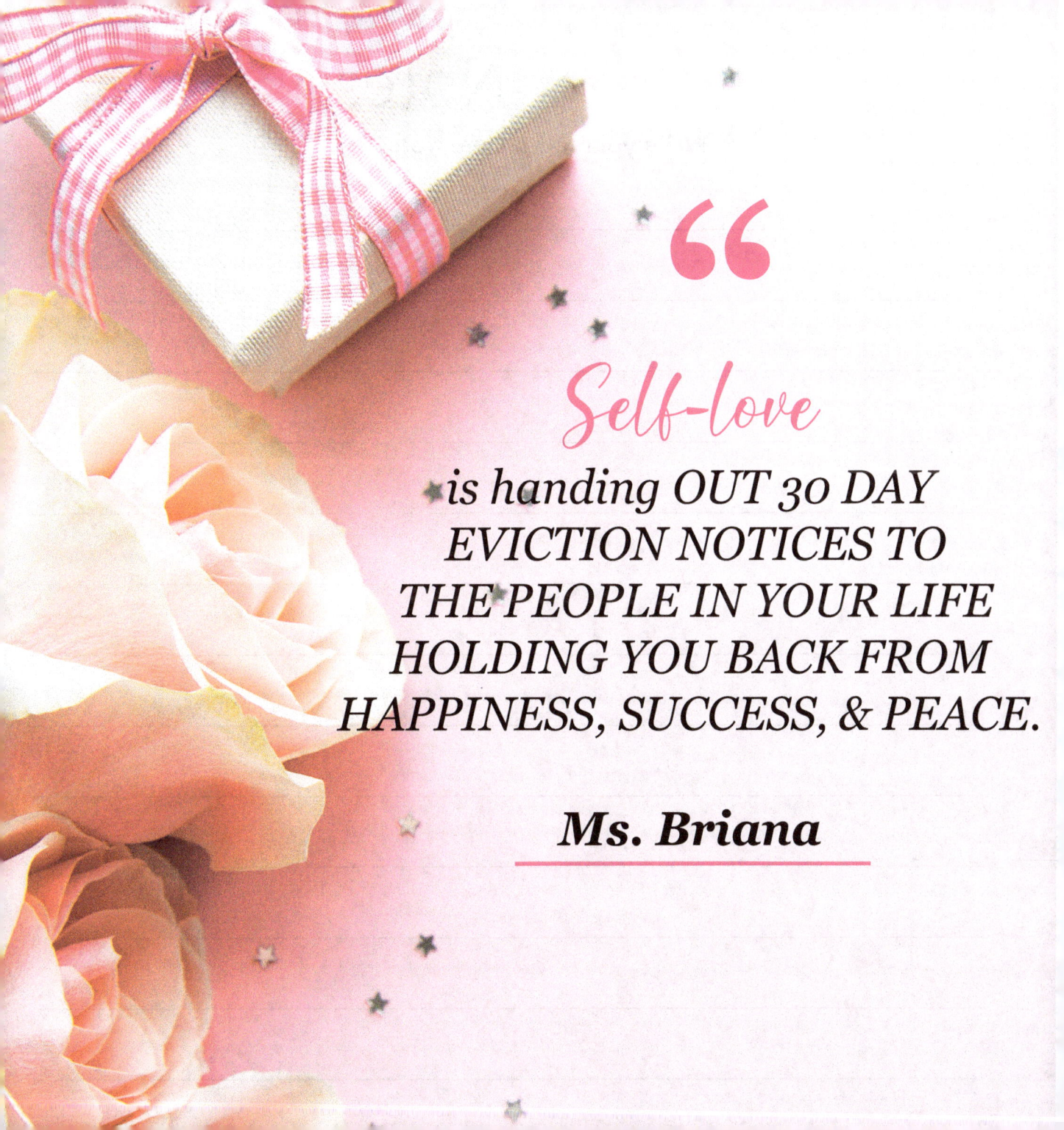

Self-Love Notes

(Write yourself a Love Note)

_____

_____

_____

_____

_____

_____

_____

_____

_____

_____

_____

> ## *Self-love*
>
> *is having peace of mind. It doesn't matter how much money you have or how many things you may have, you do not have anything if you don't have PEACE OF MIND.*
>
> — Ms. Briana

 Notes

(Write yourself a Love Note)

 # *Self-Love* Notes

(Write yourself a Love Note)

> *Self-love* is never walking on eggshells and being uncomfortable in your own space.
>
> — **Ms. Briana**

Self-Love Notes
(Write yourself a Love Note)

 Notes

(Write yourself a Love Note)

Write 5 Ways You Can Show Yourself Self-Love

1.

2.

3.

4.

5.

Am I Showing Myself *Self-Love?*

☐ YES ☐ NO

If I answered yes, how do I show myself self-love?

If I answered no, what changes do I need to make to ensure I am showing myself self-love.

Self-Love Calendar

(Use this Calendar to Track your Self Love Journey). You can add spa treatments, hanging out with friends, and even grabbing a cup of coffee and taking a walk at the park.

MONTH:

SUN	MON	TUE	WED	THU	FRI	SAT

> ## *Self-love*
>
> is when you're okay with being alone whether it's friendships or relationships that may end. You heal from them and you grow from them and never take those past issues with you into new relationships.
>
> **Ms. Briana**

Self-Love Notes
(Write yourself a Love Note)

> *Self-love* is setting boundaries for people in your life and never letting them disappoint you repeatedly.

— **Ms. Briana**

Self-Love Notes

(Write yourself a Love Note)

_____

_____

_____

_____

_____

_____

_____

_____

_____

_____

> *Self-love* is acknowledging that it's not selfish to take care of yourself!
>
> — Ms. Briana

 Notes

(Write yourself a Love Note)

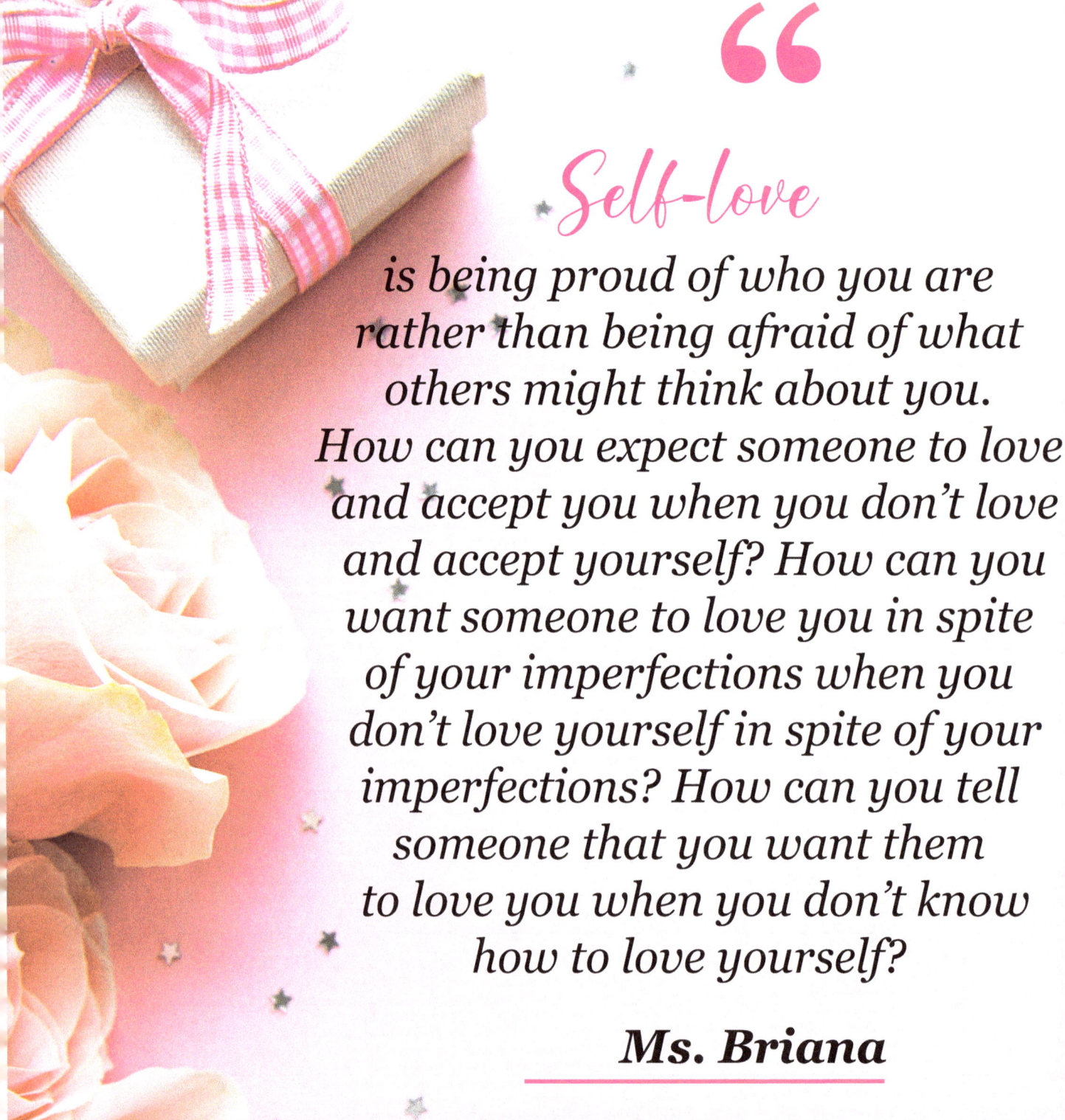

> **Self-love** is being proud of who you are rather than being afraid of what others might think about you. How can you expect someone to love and accept you when you don't love and accept yourself? How can you want someone to love you in spite of your imperfections when you don't love yourself in spite of your imperfections? How can you tell someone that you want them to love you when you don't know how to love yourself?
>
> **Ms. Briana**

Self-Love Notes

(Write yourself a Love Note)

> *Despite your relationships, you should not forget to continually love yourself. It's important to do so because you change every day, you elevate, you grow, and you become a better person every day, therefore it's essential that you stay well-informed of your growth. The same things you may want today may change tomorrow or the next day or next-year. All of this is a part of self-love. Without loving on you and knowing who you are inside and out how can you possibly tell someone else how to.*

Ms. Briana

Self-Love Notes

(Write yourself a Love Note)

_____

_____

_____

_____

_____

_____

_____

_____

_____

_____

> ## *Self-love*
>
> *is all about dating yourself taking time out from dating people or even while in a relationship continuing to date yourself. It's important to keep dating yourself because you change everyday, you elevate, you grow and you become a better person everyday so it's important that you keep up with yourself and your growth. The same things you may want today may change tomorrow or the next day or next year. Which is all apart of self love without loving on you and knowing who you are inside and out how can you possibly tell someone else how to.*

Ms. Briana

Self-Love Notes

(Write yourself a Love Note)

Self-Love Notes

(Write yourself a Love Note)

 Notes

(Write yourself a Love Note)

Write 5 Ways You Can Show Yourself Self-Love

1.

2.

3.

4.

5.

Am I Showing Myself *Self-Love?*

☐ YES ☐ NO

If I answered yes, how do I show myself self-love?

If I answered no, what changes do I need to make to ensure I am showing myself self-love.

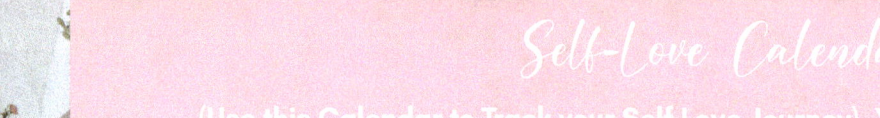

Self-Love Calendar

(Use this Calendar to Track your Self Love Journey). You can add spa treatments, hanging out with friends, and even grabbing a cup of coffee and taking a walk at the park.

MONTH:

SUN	MON	TUE	WED	THU	FRI	SAT

> ## *Self-love*
> is believing in yourself even
> when no one else does.

Ms. Briana

Self-Love Notes

(Write yourself a Love Note)

_____

_____

_____

_____

_____

_____

_____

_____

_____

_____

>

Self-love

is having the ability to
feel confident and beautiful
without needing someone
to tell you. In order to love
who you are, you cannot hate
your past mistakes and
experiences that have
helped shape
who you are as an individual.

Ms. Briana

Self-Love Notes

(Write yourself a Love Note)

> *Self-love* is the feeling of regardless how anyone else sees you or their opinion of you, still choose to be happy with who you are.

Ms. Briana

 # Self-Love Notes

(Write yourself a Love Note)

_____

_____

_____

_____

_____

_____

_____

_____

_____

_____

_____

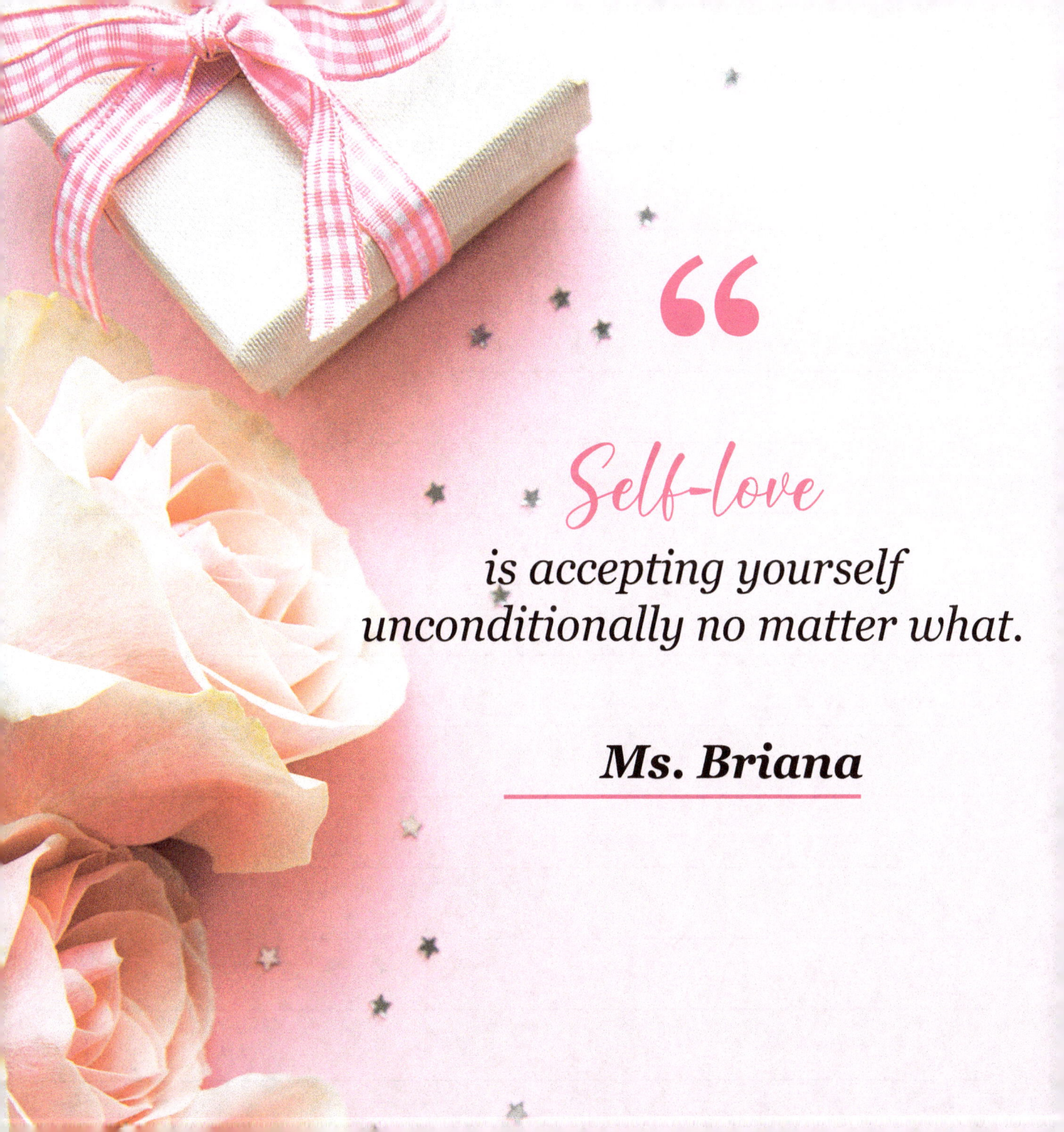

 # Notes

(Write yourself a Love Note)

_____

_____

_____

_____

_____

_____

_____

_____

_____

_____

_____

> ## *Self-love*
>
> is not letting people around you destroy you by setting boundaries and limitations. If you don't love yourself you can't possibly tell someone else how to. Not only that, you won't be good at loving anyone else.
>
> **Ms. Briana**

Self-Love Notes

(Write yourself a Love Note)

"

Self-love

starts with you and it ends with you. Demonstrate love by giving it unconditionally to yourself. And as you do, you will attract others into your life who will love you without conditions.

Ms. Briana

 Notes

(Write yourself a Love Note)

_____

_____

_____

_____

_____

_____

_____

_____

_____

_____

_____

_____

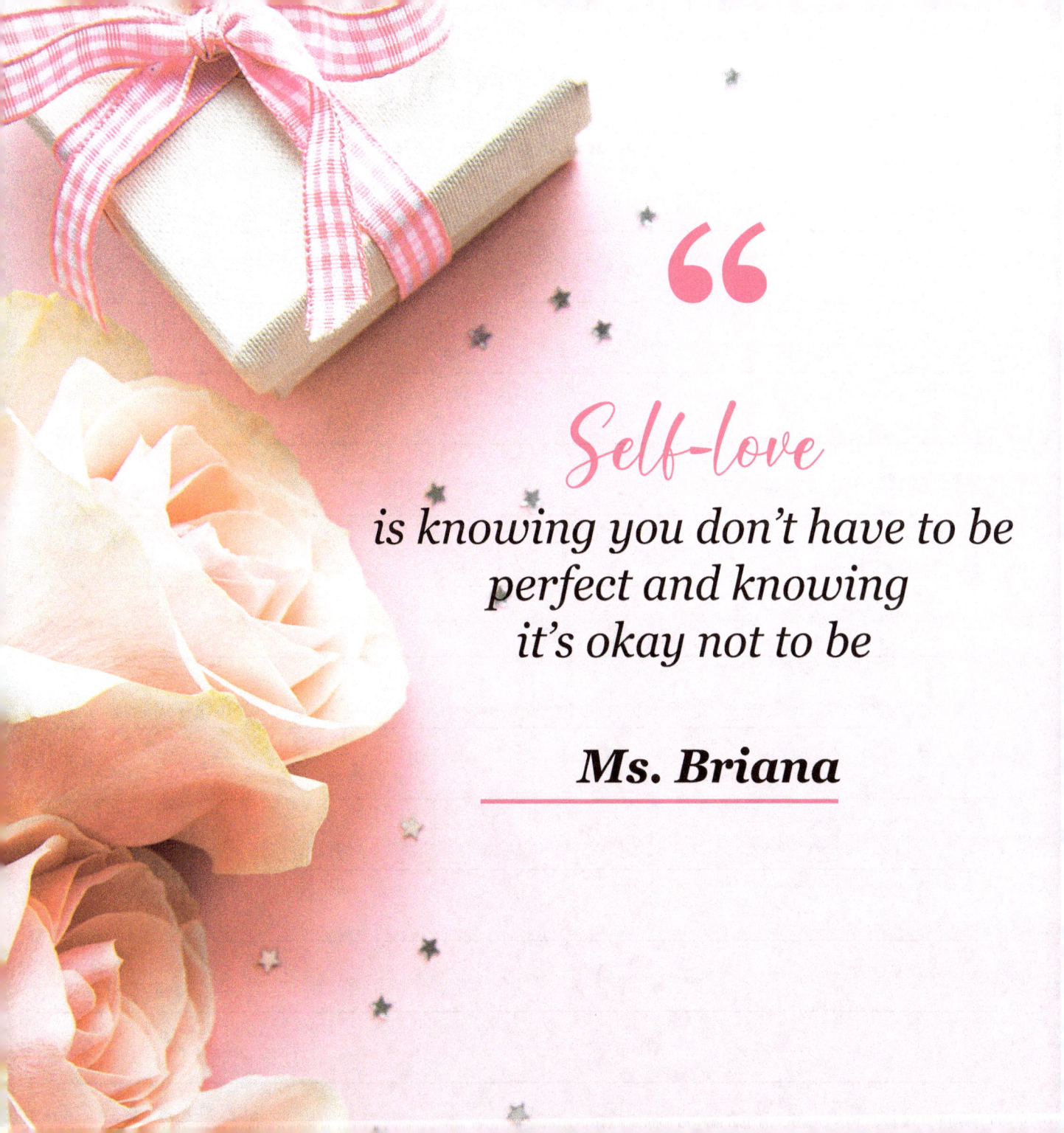

"

Self-love

is knowing you don't have to be perfect and knowing it's okay not to be

Ms. Briana

Self-Love Notes

(Write yourself a Love Note)

_____

_____

_____

_____

_____

_____

_____

_____

_____

_____

_____

_____

Write 5 Ways You Can Show Yourself Self-Love

1.

2.

3.

4.

5.

Am I Showing Myself *Self-Love?*

☐ YES ☐ NO

If I answered yes, how do I show myself self-love?

If I answered no, what changes do I need to make to ensure I am showing myself self-love.

Self-Love Calendar

(Use this Calendar to Track your Self Love Journey). You can add spa treatments, hanging out with friends, and even grabbing a cup of coffee and taking a walk at the park.

MONTH:

SUN	MON	TUE	WED	THU	FRI	SAT

"

Self-love

is also inner peace, which begins the moment you choose not to allow another person or event to control your emotions.

Ms. Briana

Self-Love Notes

(Write yourself a Love Note)

_____

_____

_____

_____

_____

_____

_____

_____

_____

_____

_____

> *Self-love is not wasting your energy trying to change opinions of you.*

Ms. Briana

Self-Love Notes

(Write yourself a Love Note)

_____

_____

_____

_____

_____

_____

_____

_____

_____

_____

> *Self-love is owning who you are, fixing your crown , and keep pushing no matter who likes it or who doesn't. You can't please everyone and you can't make everyone like you. In today's world, YOU will never win trying to be someone else in hopes of pleasing others. One thing that you will regret in life is trying to be what others would want you to be, rather than being yourself.*

Ms. Briana

 Notes

(Write yourself a Love Note)

> *Self-love* is an unconditional love no one can ever fulfill, but you.
>
> **Ms. Briana**

 **Notes**

(Write yourself a Love Note)

_____

_____

_____

_____

_____

_____

_____

_____

_____

_____

> ## *Self-love*
>
> *is being okay even when it seems like people are so judgmental of you and don't accept you for who you are.*
>
> **Ms. Briana**

Self-Love Notes

(Write yourself a Love Note)

_____

_____

_____

_____

_____

_____

_____

_____

_____

_____

> *Self-love*
> is not letting anyone let you think less of you.

Ms. Briana

Self-Love Notes

(Write yourself a Love Note)

> **Self-love** *is the feeling of being complete without needing anything or anyone to fulfill you temporarily.*
>
> — **Ms. Briana**

Self-Love Notes

(Write yourself a Love Note)

"
Self-love

is not feeling the need to be dependent on someone else building you up or being there to make you feel complete. Always remember becoming a better you will attract a better next. Your trials and tribulations are your testimonies, which turns into blessings. Always remember you hold the key to your Happiness like no one else does. So, do what makes you happy and focus on what makes you complete. Set daily goals, weekly goals, monthly goals, or even yearly goals. Setting goals will keep you motivated. Every single time you reach a goal, don't forget to celebrate you. It can be as little as dancing and singing in your room! Nobody can celebrate, uplift, and encourage you like you can do for you!

Ms. Briana

Self-Love Notes

(Write yourself a Love Note)

_____

_____

_____

_____

_____

_____

_____

_____

_____

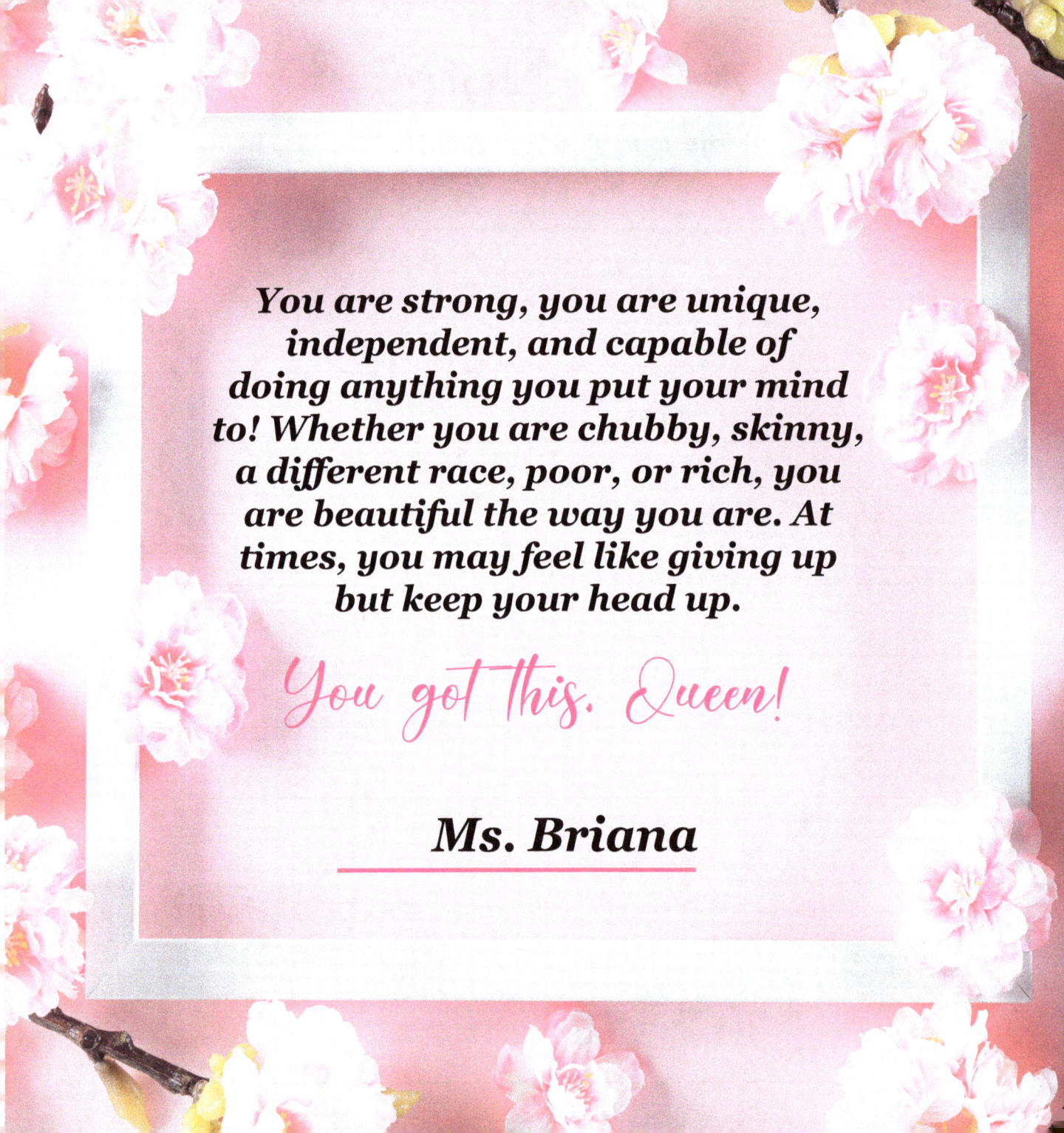

How has this *Self-Love* Journal help you?

Interested In Writing/Publishing a book?
Contact @Dr.Synovia www.a2zbookspublishing.net

www.ingramcontent.com/pod-product-compliance
Lightning Source LLC
Chambersburg PA
CBHW051805100526
44592CB00016B/2576